THE COMPLETE GUIDE TO IRISH CITIZENSHIP BY DESCENT

SORCHA BYRNE

Hello! Dia dhuit!

INTRODUCTION

Becoming an Irish Citizen is not just a legal process; it's often a heartfelt journey to connect back to your Irish roots, heritage, and identity. Whether your Irish lineage spans generations or you have recently discovered your Irish ancestry, claiming Irish citizenship is a way to formally reconnect with Ireland and its people.

WITH THIS GUIDE, YOU WILL BE ABLE TO OBTAIN YOUR IRISH CITIZENSHIP FOR LESS THAN $800 USD AND 2-4 HOURS OF TIME.

If one of your grandparents was an Irish citizen, you are eligible for Irish citizenship by descent no matter where on the globe you were born. Once an Irish citizen, you may be able to obtain an Irish passport, move to Ireland full-time, and get access to all of the European Union.

THIS GUIDE WILL WALK YOU THROUGH THE PROCESS OF OBTAINING IRISH CITIZENSHIP BY DESCENT- WITHOUT COSTING YOU THOUSANDS OF DOLLARS OR REQUIRING AN IMMIGRATION LAWYER.

Ireland recognizes and allows dual citizenship, which means that if you obtain Irish citizenship, you will not have to relinquish your current citizenship or nationality. Dual citizenship may also allow you the flexibility of having dual passports.

For many, becoming an Irish citizen isn't just about the perks, like the right to live, work, and study in Ireland and the EU. It's about embracing a culture steeped in legend, music, literature, and traditions that have enchanted the world for centuries.

Whether you are tracing your ancestry back to the rolling hills of County Kerry or the bustling streets of Dublin, this guide will walk you through exactly how to gain Irish Citizenship by descent.

SLÁINTE, *Sorcha*

CONTENTS

CHAPTER 1: ELIGIBILITY CRITERIA FOR IRISH CITIZENSHIP

- Eligibility For Irish Citizenship by Descent
- Other Paths To Citizenship
- Passing Irish Citizenship to Children
- Benefits Of Irish Citizenship

CHAPTER 2: BENEFITS OF IRISH CITIZENSHIP

- Benefits of Irish Citizenship

CHAPTER 3: HOW TO GET IRISH CITIZENSHIP BY DESCENT

- Application Process Overview
- The Complete Process For Irish Citizenship

CHAPTER 4: RESOURCES & FREQUENTLY ASKED QUESTIONS

- Online Resource Groups
- Frequently Asked Questions

Chapter 1

Eligibility Criteria For Irish Citizenship

Eligibility For Irish Citizenship By Descent

To qualify, for Irish Citizenship by Descent via the Foreign Birth Registration there are two main requirements. First, you must have at least one Irish-born grandparent. This means that one of your grandparents was born on the island of Ireland, which includes both the Republic of Ireland and Northern Ireland.

Your Irish grandmother or Irish grandfather can be alive or have passed away. There is no age limit to apply for Irish citizenship, and you don't have to live in Ireland at any time. As long as one grandparent was born in Ireland, you can live anywhere across the globe and apply for your Irish citizenship from your home.

There are some restrictions on how you can claim Irish citizenship. You can't claim citizenship based on other family members like cousins, aunts, or uncles - it must be a grandmother or grandfather.

The second requirement is that you must be of "good character". This is a somewhat vague requirement that simply requires you to be a law-abiding citizen. If you do not have any criminal convictions, you should easily meet this requirement. If you do have any criminal convictions, you may still obtain Irish citizenship by descent. The Department of Justice allows for explanations and will consider extenuating circumstances.

IF YOU HAVE AN IRISH GRANDFATHER OR GRANDMOTHER AND A CLEAR RECORD, THE PATH TO IRISH CITIZENSHIP IS SIMPLE.

This guide will help you through the application process, detailing what documents you need and where to send them. If you meet the requirements and submit the correct paperwork, gaining your Irish citizenship should be smooth sailing. And the best part? You can do it all on your own, no lawyer or immigration agency needed!

Other Paths To Citizenship

This guide will cover how to obtain Irish Citizenship by Descent, however, there are other paths to citizenship.

- If either of your parents were born in Ireland and were Irish citizens at the time of your birth, you are automatically an Irish citizen by birth.
- If you were born in Ireland before January 1st 2005, you are an Irish citizen.
- if you were born in Northern Ireland before January 1st 2005, you can choose to be an Irish citizen and apply for an Irish passport.
- If you were born on or after January 1st 2005, your Irish citizenship depends on the nationality of your parents or where they lived. If either of your parents were Irish or UK citizens at the time of your birth, and you were born in Ireland, you are automatically an Irish citizen. If you were born in Northern Ireland to an Irish or British parent, you can choose to be an Irish citizen. Additionally, If your Irish or UK citizen parent died before you were born, you are an Irish citizen by birth.
- Finally, If an Irish citizen adopted you, you may be eligible for Irish citizenship.

OTHER ADDITIONAL WAYS TO GET CITIZENSHIP CAN BE FOUND ON THE <u>IRISH CITIZENSHIP WEBSITE</u>.

Passing Irish Citizenship To Children

As of right now, you are able to pass Irish Citizenship by Descent to your children if they are born AFTER you receive your citizenship. Children born before you were registered, are not eligible to apply for Irish citizenship.

Occasionally, the Irish government reviews requirements and has explored allowing Irish Citizen to pass Irish Citizenship to their children. Follow updates from the <u>Irish Citizenship Information Center</u> to understand current laws.

Chapter 2

Benefits Of Irish Citizenship

Benefits Of Irish Citizenship

Obtaining your Irish citizenship is a gateway to a myriad of opportunities and privileges. From practical advantages such as access to healthcare and education to broader benefits like cultural identity and global mobility, Irish citizenship offers a wealth of advantages.

1. ENJOY THE RIGHT TO LIVE AND WORK IN IRELAND

Gaining your Irish citizenship gives you the right to live and work in Ireland without any restrictions. Living as an Irish citizen, you can immerse yourself in the country's rich cultural tapestry, pursue a career in Ireland without needing sponsorship, and feel a deep connection to the country of your ancestors.

2. GAIN ACCESS TO IRISH EDUCATION

If you move to Ireland as an Irish citizen, you will gain access to Ireland's world-class educational system - spanning pre-k through college and even higher degrees. Ireland is ranked in the top three of all European nations for education quality and access. Gaining Irish citizenship will allow you and your family access to an educational system that is known for academic excellence and an inclusive approach to education. Taking advantage of the Irish educational system will equip you and your children with the knowledge and skills necessary to thrive in an increasingly competitive global landscape.

3. ENJOY COMPREHENSIVE HEALTHCARE

Irish citizens enjoy comprehensive healthcare entitlements under Ireland's public health system. As an Irish citizen in Ireland, you may be able to get access to medical treatment, hospital care, and prescription medications at subsidized rates or free of charge. As an Irish citizen you will receive timely and appropriate healthcare services to address medical needs and to promote overall well-being and quality of life.

4. PARTICIPATE IN IRISH POLITICS

As Irish citizens, you will have the privilege to participate in Ireland's democratic processes, including voting in national and local elections, engaging in public discourse on social and political issues, and standing for public office. With your Irish citizenship, you can play an active role in shaping the country's future and contributing to the democratic governance of Ireland.

5. BECOME AN EU CITIZEN

Ireland's membership in the European Union offers additional benefits to Irish citizens. With Irish citizenship, you are considered an EU citizen, and have the right to live, work, and study in any EU member state, as well as access to EU consular protection and assistance when traveling abroad.

6. GAIN AN IRISH PASSPORT

One of the largest benefits of Irish citizenship is the ability to get an Irish passport. With an Irish passport, you can travel freely across the 28 EU member states without needing additional visas. An Irish passport provides holders with visa-free or visa-on-arrival access to numerous countries and territories, making travel easier, faster and less expensive.

7. UNLOCK GLOBAL CAREER OPPORTUNITIES

With Irish citizenship, you will gain access to Ireland's extensive global network and thriving economy. Irish citizenship and EU citizenship may help you secure work in Ireland without the need for sponsored visas.

8. CONNECT TO YOUR CULTURAL HERITAGE

Irish citizenship will connect you to Ireland's rich cultural heritage, history, and traditions. As an Irish citizen you may feel a sense of pride, belonging, and shared identity among the citizens of Ireland. Whether celebrating St. Patrick's Day, enjoying traditional Irish music and dance, or exploring ancient archaeological sites, Irish citizens have a deep appreciation for their cultural roots and a keen sense of belonging to the global Irish community. Citizenship fosters a sense of kinship and solidarity among individuals with Irish ancestry, regardless of their country of residence or cultural background.

Chapter 3

How To Get Irish Citizenship By Descent

Application Process Overview

The process of getting Irish Citizenship By Descent can be a bit confusing and cumbersome, but this guide will simplify the application process and save you thousands of dollars and hundreds of hours.

THE APPLICATION PROCESS WILL REQUIRE YOU TO GATHER DOCUMENTS, AND SPEND 2-4 HOURS APPLYING. THE TOTAL COST TO OBTAIN YOUR IRISH CITIZENSHIP SHOULD BE AROUND $800 USD.

☐ 1. COLLECT LINEAGE DOCUMENTS

You will need to collect documents for your grandparents, your parents, and yourself. This guide will outline everything you need. Finding the original documents may require some work; however, relatives, churches and regional Irish municipalities may be of help in order to find the right documents.

☐ 2. SUBMIT APPLICATION ONLINE

You will complete your Foreign Birth Registration online and the application will be submitted to the Irish government electronically.

☐ 3. MAIL APPLICATION & LINEAGE DOCUMENTS TO IRELAND

You will submit a printed copy of your application and all of the lineage documents to the Foreign Births Registration Section Office. To complete this step, you will need a professional, legal witness to verify your photos and watch you sign a few documents. Luckily, many people may qualify, but your witness may not be related to you. Submitting your documents will register your birth with the Irish Government.

☐ 4. WAIT

While the Irish Department of Foreign Affairs officially says it may take up to 2 years to review the documents and approve the Foreign Birth Registration, most cases take 4-8 weeks. The Irish Department of Foreign Affairs may reach out via email, mail, or phone if more information is needed.

☐ 5. CELEBRATE

Once approved, you will receive an official approval certificate from the Irish Foreign Birth Registration in the mail. As an Irish citizen, you can now apply for your Irish passport!

The Complete Process For Irish Citizenship

STEP 1. COLLECT LINEAGE DOCUMENTS

The first, and most tedious step will be to collect documents around your family's Irish ancestry. You will need to gather three types of documents- documents about you, documents about your parents, and documents about your Irish grandparents. While this may take some work, enjoy learning more about your parents' and grandparents' histories. Some of these documents will need to be notarized which you will complete in a later step.

The application requires a copy of a state-issued ID's for you and your Irish parent. This can be a copy of your passport, drivers license, or a national identity card. This copy must be certified as a true copy of the original by a notary.

1. DOCUMENTS ABOUT YOU

Gather these documents pertaining to you:

- Your original birth certificate

- Your original marriage certificate - if applicable

- Your original divorce papers - if applicable

- A certified photocopy of your passport or state issued ID (a passport, driver's license or national identity card)

- 4 passport photos - 2 must be signed, stamped, and dated by your witness

- 2 original documents showing proof of address- these can be a utility bill, bank statement, or lease (these cannot be photocopies)

2. DOCUMENTS ABOUT YOUR IRISH PARENT

Gather the following documents of your parent who has Irish ancestry. If both parents are Irish, gather the documents of both parents.

- The original birth certificate of your parent
- The original marriage certificate of your parent showing their parents
- A certified photocopy of your parent's passport or state issued ID (a passport, driver's license, or national identity card)
- The original death certificate of your parent - if applicable
- The original divorce certificate of your parent - if applicable

3. DOCUMENTS ABOUT YOUR IRISH BORN GRANDPARENT

The most difficult part of getting your Irish citizenship may be finding the documents of your Irish grandparent. You may search for your documents in churches, local towns, or hospitals in Ireland.

- The original birth certificate of your grandparent which includes their parents' information
- The original marriage certificate of your grandparent
- A certified photocopy of your parent's passport or state issued ID (a passport, drivers license or national identity card)
- The original Death Certificate of your grandparent
- The original Divorce Certificate of your grandparent

Finding the original birth certificate for your grandparent may be difficult especially if they were born in a rural part of Ireland. In fact, some parts of Ireland have never issued birth certificates. Instead, a baptismal certificate may be used as a birth certificate if it qualifies. To use a baptismal certificate in place of a birth certificate, you must first search for your grandparent's birth certificate through the General Registrar's Office. The Registrar's Office will search for a birth certificate and if they cannot find one, they will send you a letter stating there is no birth certificate on record. Include the letter from the General Registrar's Office with the baptismal certificate that includes the church stamp on it in your application.

STEP 2. SUBMIT THE FOREIGN BIRTH APPLICATION

After you have gathered your lineage documents, set aside an hour to submit your online citizenship application.

To complete your application you will need:

- A computer connected to the internet
- Your lineage documents
- A credit card to pay the ~$300 fee
    (Visa, Mastercard and American Express are accepted)
- Access to a printer to print a hard copy of your application

First, visit the Foreign Birth Registration at https://fbr.dfa.ie/finprod/fbr301.xsp website via the Irish Department of Foreign Affairs. In the General tab, you will select Foreign BIrth Registration. An outline of all questions asks on the FOREIGN BIRTH APPLICATION QUESTIONS can be found in the RESOURCE section of this guide.

An Roinn Gnóthaí Eachtracha
Department of Foreign Affairs

NÁISIÚN
FOREIGN BIRTH REGISTRATION

Accessibility

Language Select   Gaeilge

| General | Applicant | Parent | Grandparent | Contact Details | Submit Application |

Select country of residence

Country	UNITED STATES OF AMERICA ∨ *
Region	Illinois ∨ *

Age of person whose birth is to be registered

◉ 18 or over   ○ Under 18

Please indicate the citizenship category to which the applicant's parent belongs

Important: Please note that this question relates to how the **PARENT** acquired Irish citizenship

○ Born abroad to a parent born in Ireland   ○ Naturalisation   ○ Post nuptial declaration   ◉ Foreign births registration   ○ Born abroad and adopted by an Irish citizen

Next

Once you have completed the Foreign Birth Application you must print a hard copy, which will be mailed, and submit the form online. You can print via a web page or via a PDF.

ONCE YOU HAVE REVIEWED THE INFORMATION PRINT 3 COPIES OF THE APPLICATION: 1 COPY WILL BE MAILED TO IRELAND, KEEP 2 COPIES OF THE APPLICATION FOR YOUR RECORDS

As the final step, you must submit your application online. After reviewing the printed copies select YES if your application is correct.

After hitting submit, you will be taken to the payment page. You will need to pay €278 Euro or ~$300 US dollars to submit the application. Congratulations on submitting your application online!

STEP 3. MAIL YOUR APPLICATION & LINEAGE DOCUMENTS TO IRELAND

To submit your application you will need: your lineage documents, your printed application form, and a professional witness or notary to witness your signatures on the documents.

YOU WILL NEED A LEGAL WITNESS TO SIGN SEVERAL DOCUMENTS.

A notary must sign the copy of your passport as well as the copy of your parent's passport. You can find a notary by searching online, at your local bank, at a law firm, library, or real estate firms. The notary may charge a small fee, usually less than $50 US dollars, for their services.

You will also need a legal witness to fill out section E of the application, watch you sign your passport photos, watch you sign the application, and provide their contact information for a potential follow up. This person can be the same person as your notary or it can be a clergy, priest, police officer, lawyer, medical doctor, judge or bank manager. It may not be a family member. After your witness has signed everything, review your application with the checklist on the next page.

SEND YOUR DOCUMENTS TO:
FOREIGN BIRTHS REGISTRATION SECTION
PO BOX 13003
BALBRIGGAN, CO. DUBLIN, IRELAND

Please note, your documents will be returned to you via mail, however, it can be nerve wracking to send sensitive, personal documents abroad. It is recommended to make three copies of all of your documents: one to mail to Ireland, a second set of copies should be kept easily accessible to answer questions or re-submit. Finally, keep a third set of copies in a safe or lockbox. When mailing to Ireland, it is important to mail all documents via FedEx with tracking. Sending your documents to Ireland with tracking will cost around $200.

The Irish government will return all of your certificates to the address on your application form. You do not need to send a prepaid envelope for any of your documents, but you will need to be home to sign and to receive the documents.

THE COMPLETE FOREIGN BIRTH REGISTRATION APPLICATION CHECKLIST

☐ Your original birth certificate

☐ Your original marriage certificate (if applicable)

☐ Your original divorce papers (if applicable)

☐ 1 copy of your Passport or ID – must be notarized

☐ 4 passport photos – 2 must be signed, stamped and dated by a witness

☐ 3 original documents showing proof of current residence – these can be a utility bill, bank statement or lease.

☐ The original Birth Certificate of your parent

☐ The original Marriage Certificate of your parents

☐ 1 copy of parent's passport or ID – must be notarized

☐ The original Death Certificate of your parent (if applicable)

☐ The original Divorce Certificate of your parent (if applicable)

☐ The original Birth Certificate of your grandparent

☐ The original Marriage Certificate of your grandparent

☐ 1 copy of the grandparent's passport or ID– must be notarized

☐ The original Death Certificate of your grandparent (if applicable)

☐ The original Divorce Certificate of your grandparent (if applicable)

☐ Your printed and signed Foreign Birth Registration Application

STEP 4. WAIT

While it can be hard to wait, now that you have submitted your application there is nothing left to do! The Department of Foreign Affairs states that it may take up to 2 years to receive your Foreign Birth Registration. However, traditionally, the process takes 4-8 weeks.

The Foreign Birth Registration may reach out via email to ask for additional information or documentation. You may be asked to resubmit documents including photos, consent forms, or other documents. When requesting documents, the email will include a link to submit the required documents. If the link expires, you can <u>request a new link</u> at https://passportresubmissions.dfa.ie/resubmission. You will receive an email with a new link within 2-5 days.

Also, while you may want to use this time to get your Irish passport, you cannot apply for an Irish passport yet. You must first register your birth via the Foreign Birth Registration which will then give you Irish Citizenship. After getting your Irish Citizenship, you may apply for a passport.

STEP 5. CELEBRATE

Once approved, you will receive an official Irish Foreign Birth Registration in the mail. Celebrate your Irish citizenship with family and friends over a Guiness. As an Irish citizen, you can now apply for your Irish passport!

Chapter 4
Resources &
Frequently Asked
Questions

Irish Government Resource

The Irish government has many details and additional information on their website at https://www.ireland.ie/en/dfa/citizenship/. Additionally, details around how to register a foreign birth can be found found via the Born Abroad link at https://www.ireland.ie/en/dfa/citizenship/born-abroad/registering-a-foreign-birth/

To begin your application click here or visit https://fbr.dfa.ie/eseries/fbr301.xsp

Please note, the US embassy is not able to offer support in gaining your Irish citizenship.

If you need additional help the Irish Foreign Birth Registration office has created a Customer Service Hub to provide additional support. The Customer Service Hub is available by telephone and reachable at +353-1-568-3331. Agents are available to help from Monday to Friday, 9am to 4.30pm Irish Standard Time.

Additionally, you may chat with a customer Service agent via WebChat or at https://www.ireland.ie/en/dfa/passports/contact-us/#webchat which is open Monday through Friday, 9am to 4.30pm Irish Standard Time. The webchat will only work when the button is green, if it is gray refresh the page.

Resource Groups

The process of obtaining your Irish citizenship can be confusing, fortunately many online communities have thousands of others also working to get Irish citizenship. These communities can be a great place to ask questions, seek clarity and learn from other applicants. Here are some of our favorite online communities for obtaining Irish citizenship.

Facebook Groups
- Americans applying for Irish citizenship
- Irish Citizenship Application
- Irish Naturalisation Citizenship Online Process to receiving Passport 2024
- Irish Family Ancestry Research and Help

Reddit Community at https://www.reddit.com/r/IrishCitizenship/

Many immigration law firms will also advertise services to help immigrate to Ireland or help with Irish citizenship. Often time these services are very expensive and take a long time. They may or may not be able to secure your Irish citizenship.

Foreign Birth Application

Here is an outline of all questions required in the Foreign Birth Application Form:

- **General Tab**
  - Country of residence
  - Age of person whose birth is to be registered
  - Please indicate the citizenship category to which the applicant's parent belongs
- **Applicant Tab-** Details of the person whose birth is to be registered
  - First name on birth certificate
  - Last name on birth certificate
  - Date of Birth
  - Gender
  - First Name if different from birth certificate
  - Last Name if different from birth certificate
  - Country of birth
  - Place of birth
  - Marital Status
  - Mother's Maiden Last name
- **Parent Tab-** Details of the parent whom Irish citizenship is said to be derived
  - First name on birth certificate
  - Last name on birth certificate
  - Date of Birth
  - Gender
  - First Name if different from birth certificate
  - Last Name if different from birth certificate
  - Country of birth
  - Place of birth
  - Marital Status
  - Mother's Maiden Last name
  - Did this person ever make a "declaration of alienage" (renouncing Irish citizenship).

Foreign Birth Application (continued)

- **Grandparent Tab**- Details of the grandparent born in Ireland
  - First name on birth certificate
  - Last name on birth certificate
  - Date of Birth
  - Gender
  - First name if different from birth certificate
  - Last Name if different from birth certificate
  - Country of birth
  - Mother's Maiden Last name
  - Marital Status
  - Did this person ever make a "declaration of alienage" (renouncing Irish citizenship).
- **Contact Details**
  - Mailing address
  - Daytime phone number
  - Home phone number
  - Email address

THE COMPLETE FOREIGN BIRTH REGISTRATION APPLICATION CHECKLIST

- ☐ Your original birth certificate
- ☐ Your original marriage certificate (if applicable)
- ☐ Your original divorce papers (if applicable)
- ☐ 1 copy of your Passport or ID - must be notarized
- ☐ 4 passport photos - 2 must be signed, stamped and dated by a witness
- ☐ 3 original documents showing proof of current residence - these can be a utility bill, bank statement or lease.
- ☐ The original Birth Certificate of your parent
- ☐ The original Marriage Certificate of your parents
- ☐ 1 copy of parent's passport or ID – must be notarized
- ☐ The original Death Certificate of your parent (if applicable)
- ☐ The original Divorce Certificate of your parent (if applicable)
- ☐ The original Birth Certificate of your grandparent
- ☐ The original Marriage Certificate of your grandparent
- ☐ 1 copy of the grandparent's passport or ID- must be notarized
- ☐ The original Death Certificate of your grandparent (if applicable)
- ☐ The original Divorce Certificate of your grandparent (if applicable)
- ☐ Your printed and signed Foreign Birth Registration Application

Frequently Asked Questions

How much will it cost to get Irish citizenship?
The entire process of obtaining your Irish Citizenship can be completed for around $600. While this is an investment, applying for your Irish Citizenship on your own will save you thousands of dollars in legal fees.

Here is a breakdown in estimated costs. Again, all costs are in USD and approximate.

Cost To Find and Obtain All Required Original Documents ~$100
Irish Citizenship Application ~$300 USD
Mailing Documents via FedEx ~$200.00

How long will it take to get my Irish citizenship?
The Irish Department of Foreign Affairs states that is may take up to 2 years to receive your Foreign Birth Registration. However, traditionally the process takes 4-8 weeks.

Can I apply for the Foreign Birth Registration and passport at the same time? No, you cannot apply for an irish passport until you are an Irish citizen. You must first register your birth via the Foreign Birth Registration which will then give you Irish Citizenship. After that you may apply for a passport. We've created a helpful guide to help you through that process.

Can my sibling and I apply for Foreign Birth Registration jointly?
Yes, you can use the same set of papers and supporting documents for both applications. Just enclose the two separate application forms in one envelope and send it to us with a letter saying that some of the documents apply to both applications. This only applies if you are resident in the same country when applying.

F.A.Q.s Continued

My grandparent was born in Ireland but neither of my parents have Irish Passports. Can I still apply for Irish citizenship?

Yes. An application for Irish citizenship through Foreign Births Registration can be submitted by any person with a grandparent born on the island of Ireland.

My Grandparent was born before 1864, when Irish civil birth registrations began –what documents can I use?

If your grandparent was born before civil birth certificats were issued you can apply using your grandparent's Baptismal certificate.

You can search for birth certificates through the General Registrar's Office. If they cannot find a record of the birth (an original birth certificate of your relative), try the local church where your relative was born. Local churches recorded births with Baptismal Certificates.

When applying, send the original copy of the church. baptismal certificate with the church stamp on it. Also send the note that you will receive from the General Registrar's Office stating that the General Registrar's Office could not find the birth certificate.

Note, there may be discrepancies between the original birth certificate date and the baptismal certificate date. Since home births were common in Ireland, the Irish often baptized the infant before recording the actual birth with the registrar due to the considerable distance from the registrar's office. In Ireland, many church records were also lost, destroyed, or damaged by fire.

FAQ Continued

What should I do if I am not approved for Irish Citizenship?

While many Foreign Birth Registrations are approved, there is a chance that your request for Foreign Birth Registration is denied. If this happens, you will receive a letter of refusal that will detail the reasons why the application was denied. You can appeal this decision within 6 weeks of the date you receive the letter by writing to the Foreign Birth Registration Appeals Officer.

In the letter, provide why you believe you should be granted a Foreign Birth Registration and address the reason for denial. Mail that letter to
Foreign Birth Registration Appeals Officer
Foreign Births Registration Section
PO Box 13003
Balbriggan, Co Dublin
Ireland

If you are still denied, you may write to the Office of the Ombudsman via mail or email. Please include a detailed letter of why you believe your application and appeal were denied. You can reach the office of the Ombudsman online by clicking on the 'Make A Complaint' link at ombudsman.ie or via mail at
Office of the Ombudsman
6 Earlsfort Terrace
Dublin 2
D02 W773
Tel: +353 1 639 5600

Further contact details for the Ombudsman are at ombudsman.ie/contact.